# IN BETWEEN SUICIDES

## One Man's Journey Into Bad Health

Billy Wright

www.trafford.com
**North America & international**
toll-free: 1 888 232 4444 (USA & Canada)
fax: 812 355 4082

# CHAPTER NUMBER 1

When I was twenty-six, and six feet, two inches tall, I weighed 155 pounds. That was when I was diagnosed as type 1 diabetic. I was not fat. I was not overweight. I certainly was not obese. I didn't drink alcohol, smoke cigarettes, nor do drugs. In fact, I was a health nut and had been a fitness enthusiast for years.

But a mere two months earlier, I had weighed 193 pounds. And for my height, my weight was target. So in two months, I had lost thirty-eight pounds—a half pound per day. Before I had lost my energy and strength, I had worked out with weights six days a week. I ran up to five miles every other morning and walked five miles every other morning. I also exercised plyometrics daily.

As a fitness enthusiast, I had already studied and knew about how our bodies' digestive system works in making and using carbohydrates, protein, and fat for nutrition. But I didn't know anything about diabetes, and how it worked, or rather didn't work. If I had known, it would've been easier to recognize the symptoms I had.

I had been tired, even exhausted. I was very thirsty, drank liquids by the gallons, but remained dehydrated all the time. I was using the restroom and urinating every twenty minutes or so, day and night. For example, I would drink a full two-liter bottle of horchata, then, when someone else was in the restroom, and I couldn't wait, I'd pee into the empty bottle, and almost fill it back up with pee.

I didn't know what was wrong with me, but some people told me that I had "valley fever," which is a real thing that some people get when they move to the Valley of the Sun. It's actually a mold spore thing, but rumor had it that people got it from the heat when they first moved into Phoenix and the surrounding areas, which I had done several months earlier.

I had recently started a new job and was trying to wait on seeing a doctor until my first ninety days had been completed and I got my new health insurance. In the meantime, my vision was blurry, and it was difficult to see traffic lights and signs, especially at night. I always had high-pressure headaches, which never stopped, and only seemed to get worse.

It was awful at work where I had to take a break every twenty minutes or so to use the restroom. Then one day, I fell out at work and crashed my order selector/forklift into a metal shelf and fell to the warehouse floor. My bosses decided not to fire me if I went to a doctor to get checked out before I came back to work.

So I went home and called my mother's doctor to make an appointment. I got an appointment for the next day and went to see the doctor. Almost as soon as he saw me and heard my symptoms, he diagnosed me with diabetes. I said I didn't know anything about diabetes. So he started telling me about it.

Carbohydrates, which are found in fruits, vegetables, and grains, form sugar that our bodies use for energy.

Carbohydrates can be complex (which digest slower) and simple (which digest faster), but they both turn into the same sugars which are our bodies' only source of energy. The liver can also convert both fat and protein into sugar. As well as excess sugar into fat for storage for future use as reconverted sugar.

But our bodies can't use sugar, or glucose, as it's called in our bloodstream, without insulin. Insulin is a hormone produced by the pancreas after we eat food, and our brains tell the pancreas how much insulin it needs to produce based on how much glucose we consumed. The insulin then locks the glucose away into muscle and brain cells for use in those areas.

Glucose levels can be checked by a glucose monitor, and the number of target is 100. One hundred is the median goal. Seventy-five to 125 is the safe area. Any reading above 125 is considered "high sugars," and any reading below 75 is considered "low sugars." Either too high or too low can result in comas, and even deaths.

As a diabetic (type 1), the pancreas doesn't produce insulin anymore. So they have to inject insulin, which used to be made from porcine (pork/pigs) or bovine (cows) sources but are now all synthetic, created in a petri dish. Type 2 diabetics have pancreases that still produce insulin, but their bodies don't lock the insulin away like it should.

They usually don't have to take insulin injections, but they do have to take pills (like glucophage) to help their body absorb insulin. Now there is a type 3 diabetic, but they're not called type 3 like they should be. They get the least amount of attention and deserve more. Their pancreases don't get the signal from the brain to only produce a certain correlating amount of insulin, and so it produces too much insulin. It's called hypoglycemia, but as that's the end result, it would be more accurate to call them *hyper*insulinists not *hypo*glycemics.

For diabetics who can't properly lock away the sugar in their bloodstream, the sugars simply build up in the bloodstream and become what they call "high sugars." With high sugars, the body begins to use all water in the body to make urine to "float off" the sugars from the bloodstream through urine, leaving the body dehydrated.

That's why I was constantly thirsty, always hydrating but always dehydrated, plus using the restroom all the time. High sugars also expand blood vessels and change eyesight in the eyeballs. That's how the vision gets blurry. Given time, it can also result in damage to the extremities like fingers and toes, feet and hands, plus cuts that won't heal.

On the other hand, while high sugars are called *hyper*glycemic, low sugars are called *hypo*glycemics, and low blood sugars can occur when too much insulin is injected. When sugars drop too low in the body, the effects can be detrimental. When sugars in the body's cells empty first, hands and arms can spasm wildly, uncontrollably.

In legs, they can trip, stumble, weaken, and give way, causing the diabetic to fall down. In the face, like in the lips or tongue, speech can be slurred and taste buds lost. But when the brain sugars drop too low, either first or last, there can be a lack of intelligence, bad decisions, and even blackouts, or unconsciousness, even comatose. At worst, the heart can be stopped and result in a fatal heart attack.

But while still alive, some of the problems are not even medical nor mental but emotional—in personality. Low sugars can change a person's attitude and behavior, including speech, resulting in a person saying and acting differently than normally. And it's usually negatively, arguing, fighting, and even being violent. It's very common for diabetics to be argumentative and even combative, even when people are trying to help them.

I've had many too many "sugar-lows," and to share them, I'm writing different episodes in between chapters that I've called "interludes."

## INTERLUDE NUMBER 1

One time, I had "sugar-lowed" in the living room one evening. I was especially difficult for my sister to help me, which is unfortunately common for diabetics. We can even be combative, which I was that evening. I started out just running from the paramedics when my sister called them for assistance.

When I heard their radios outside the apartment and getting closer, I jumped up and ran from the living room into my bedroom. But when two of them followed me in there, I had nowhere else to run. Ignorantly, I ran into the open closet, smashing into the back wall, knocking clothes down, and breaking plastic hangers.

They helped me back up, but then I charged them like a football player and blasted past them. I ran into the other three of them in the living room, and they made a line with interlocked arms to block me. I pushed into the blockage, but they wrestled me to the floor, with four of them on my arms and legs, and the other one to start checking my blood sugar levels on my right hand's fingers.

Once he had proven that it was low, he started an intravenous (IV) in the back of my right hand, and started injecting glucose into my system. It was very challenging at the time, but I can laugh about it now.

# CHAPTER NUMBER 2

After telling me all of that, which took a while and was probably the longest doctor appointment I had ever had, the doctor then asked me what kind of health insurance I had. When I told him that I didn't have any, which was why I had waited so long to see anyone about it, he paled. He called in the intake nurse and told her to take all paperwork that there was about my visit and shred it all—leave no record that I had been there at all.

He told me that if I got diagnosed with diabetes before I had health insurance, then my diabetes would be a preexisting condition and then "no health insurance company would touch me with a hundred-foot pole." He told me to get health insurance, and then come back, and we would continue treatment. So I went home and called Blue Cross/Blue Shield from an information packet I had had from a job before the latest one.

The lady that I spoke with there said that I still had insurance coverage; it was just that no one had activated it. So she "pushed a button," and I had coverage. I immediately called the doctor's office back and told them that I needed to schedule an appointment and got one for the very next day.

When I went back to the doctor's office, the intake nurse asked for my insurance card, and I gave her the one from the information packet from BC/BS. She swiped the card and made a phone call, then handed it back and confirmed that I had been approved. Then I saw the doctor, and he immediately wrote me prescriptions for insulin, syringes, a glucose monitor, and test strips for the monitor.

They had drawn blood the day before, so they knew the lab work results, but he wanted me to start checking my own blood with him so I would get practice at it. From there, he taught me how to count carbohydrates and wanted me to cut calories down to 1,800 calories per day to see if that would bring my blood sugars down.

I had a 183 blood sugar count when they first did lab work on me, which is pretty high, but it could be a lot worse. And over the next several weeks, even though I cut my calories down to only one thousand calories per day, my sugars continued to rise, slowly but surely. My doctor said that it was obvious by then that I was type 1 for sure and I would have to start taking insulin injections.

But then, six weeks later, another doctor showed up and told me that the doctor that I had been seeing was a substitute while he had been on vacation. I met with both of them, together, and the one who had been on vacation said that it was still too early to diagnose me as type 1. He said that he would keep me on diabetic pills and keep cutting calories for me.

I couldn't cut any more calories though, and I was always hungry from all of the calories that I had already cut. So I told them that I was going to go with the original doctor and start taking insulin. When I got home though, I returned a phone call to BC/BS and found out that they had just finally gotten my first claims.

The lady whom I spoke with told me that I didn't have insurance and wouldn't unless I paid a $1,500 per month premium and then a $500 per appointment deductible. And that really defeated the purpose when I probably wouldn't spend more than a couple hundred dollars per month without it.

I felt the weight of the world on my shoulders after that. I had already been diagnosed with a disease that could be terminal. In fact, the life expectancy of a diabetic is in the fifties versus the seventies, like normal people. And if you have diabetes, then you will die from diabetes, short of a car wreck, lightning strike, or cancer. Even though the cause of death will be listed as heart attack or whatever diabetes caused for death.

So learning that was already weighing on me, and now, the fact that I didn't have health insurance, and never would, was just that much heavier. It was too much. I was very depressed. But from there, I went to a pharmacy where I had already purchased the glucose monitor and test strips and paid cash for the insulin and syringes. I also found out that anybody, even without a doctor's prescription, can buy insulin and syringes.

All by myself, I took my first injection of insulin. It was the first of many. Almost from the beginning, I have found it very difficult to regulate my sugar levels. My sugar's roller coaster—high and low—and the only time it's on target is temporarily on the way up or down between highs and lows.

I got a new job that had a loophole for health insurance because they would cover a preexisting condition as long as one hadn't seen a doctor for that condition for at least one year. So all I had to do was not go to the hospital for a year since I wasn't seeing a doctor anyway, and then I got the health insurance coverage that I needed so badly.

## INTERLUDE NUMBER 2

One time, I started sugar-lowing, and my sister handed me a plastic tumbler of chocolate milk. I walked from the kitchen into the living room with the cup. I stood in front of the television and tried to watch something. But then my arms started "spasming," and the milk started splashing out—all over the TV, VCR, digital box, and the cabinet holding it all. It was very messy, and it took me a lot of time to clean up later. But now I can laugh about it.

# CHAPTER NUMBER 3

The worst time that I sugar-lowed was one time in Flagstaff, Arizona, when I actually died. In fact, my heart stopped twice that day. I had been so down and depressed that I was going to lose my life early to diabetes that I had become suicidal. I know it's ironic. Also, I honestly thought that I could become an angel, and protect and help others.

I had been practicing taking injections of too much insulin to see how they would affect me. The plan was that I would just fall asleep and not wake up, as was common for many diabetics. But I quickly found out that when I got close to dying, adrenaline would rush through my system, my heart rate would race, and I would wake up— every time.

Until finally, one night at a motel in Flagstaff, where I was working, I woke up but didn't rush to "sugar up." I, instead, went to the restroom and looked in the mirror. With my hands gripped tightly on the edges of the sink and my forehead resting against the mirror, I stared myself in the eyes until the adrenaline rush crashed and faded away. Then I smoked a last cigarette, then collapsed into bed, and went back to sleep.

That was it. It was over. I had started to die. And then all I had to do was finish it. Then I'd be an angel. Free to fly. And visit people I loved, and be there for them, to help them, better than heavenly angels helped people, which they didn't. But I would. And then I would—

But then my cell phone rang! And it woke me up. I could barely move. Barely answer the phone. But I couldn't speak. It was my sister calling me with her cell phone from Phoenix, and when she could hear me trying to talk but not talking, she told our mom to use the home phone to call 911 for Flagstaff.

911 operators in Phoenix called 911 operators in Flagstaff, and they sent paramedics to my motel. In Arizona, the primary paramedics are firefighters who stay busy in between fire calls by operating as paramedics. Then there are private emergency medical technicians (EMT) who drive ambulances to transport patients to emergency rooms (ER). They are secondary paramedics.

The firefighters had the motel manager unlock the door to my room. When they came into the room, a couple of them laughed, and one of them said, "Looks like another druggie had a bad night." My nose had bled all over my face and chest. I guess that I looked more like a druggie than a diabetic with the blood. I don't know.

But then another of them said that the caller had said that I was diabetic. Another of them was asking me questions and I was answering them: what day it was, what year it was, who the president was. And I was watching them as they all got around the bed. Then, one of them, a guy with a mustache, told me to open my eyes. I told him that my eyes were open. But he didn't respond to me.

He had already leaned over me, then he reached down to my eyes, and with his thumb and forefinger, he opened my eyelid. But I could see him the same way both before and after him opening my eye. He then told the others that I was unconscious and unresponsive, and my pupils were fully dilated.

I thought to myself, *How can they say I'm unconscious and unresponsive? Why did he tell me to open my eyes? I am conscious and responding, and my eyes are open.* Were they right though? And was I having an out-of-body experience? But all they did was check my blood, and then the checker told another that I had a twenty-three.

From there, they hooked me up to an IV and injected a D50 (50 percent dextrose/sugar) into my veins. Then they carried me outside and put me on a gurney then into an ambulance and off toward a hospital. But on the way in the ambulance, hooked up to a heart monitor, my heart stopped, and an EMT pumped another D50 into my veins. It restarted my heart after a few missed beats.

They got me into the ER and onto a bed just before my heart stopped again. But this time it stayed stopped. The ER doctor injected a tube of D100 (100 percent dextrose) into the IV, then followed it up with a tube of saline solution to push the sugar through. Then he got two defibrillator paddles and rubbed them together to warm them up. Then he put the two paddles on my chest, on either side of my heart, and called out, "Clear!"

The defibrillator jolt jump-started my heart, which pulled the dextrose into my heart and into my brain. But the last thing that I had heard was the vital signs monitor. My heart flatlined, and that steady beep was the last thing I heard as my vision swirled into blackness. My brain cells that were emptying out of sugar and life were recognizing the cells that were already empty and dark. And I knew that I was dying.

This darkness was not what I thought death would be like. I thought the soul or spirit would live beyond the body after the body died. But all I had was emptiness. I couldn't move. I couldn't speak or communicate. I was afraid that, at best, I would be trapped inside my dead body, first in a coffin and then on the ground. I was scared. There was no life after death for me.

But then I started to see around me again. And then I felt delayed reaction of pain in my IV site from when they had pumped the dextrose in. Then I felt more pain there from the saline solution. Then I felt the surge from the defibrillator sharply emanating through my chest, then down and out through my arms and legs. And I could hear my heart beating regularly on the vital signs monitor. I was alive again!

The only other person in the ER then was an intake nurse who, according to her, was calling on the phone up to the intensive care unit (ICU) to transfer my patient files before transferring me up there. She covered all that I've covered so far, plus she added that my blood sugar levels had gone from a twenty-three in the hotel room to an eighteen in the ambulance to an eleven in the ER just before my heart stopped the second time.

She said that the second time my heart stopped, it had stayed stopped for a total of three minutes and forty-two seconds. Then she followed it all up with "And now he appears to be comatose. He's not brain dead though it was a close call, but he is in a coma."

But then another nurse came in to check on me and saw that my eyes were opening. "Oh, so you're coming back around now. That's good." She called out to the intake nurse about me, and then asked me how I was feeling. I told her that I was very cold. And she said that she could see that I was shaking. So then she got me a warm blanket out of a cabinet. When she put it on me, I started to warm up. It felt good.

From there, the morning shift doctor, a lady, came to talk to me. She practically whispered. She wanted to know what had happened to make that episode so much worse than usual. I told her that I had taken more insulin than usual to eat some cake but then fell asleep watching TV and didn't eat it.

That was because I had the remains of a full dinner from KFC in my room, including a chocolate chip cake. And I had left the TV on and was listening to the beginning of *X-Files* on that Sunday night when I first fell asleep from sleeping pills. I told her about the sleeping pills too, though I didn't tell her that I had taken six pills. They were generic Benadryl antihistamine tablets.

She said that they knew all of that because the firefighters had reported what was in the room, and from the results of my lab work for my blood. But it still wouldn't explain what all had happened to me. But I stuck to my story. So she said that since they had brought my sugars back up, and stabilized me, they would soon be letting me go.

After all that I had gone through, I just wasn't ready to go back to normal life yet, so I whispered back to her that I had deliberately overdosed on three syringes of one hundred units each, for a total of three hundred units of regular insulin, plus the six pills. She said that they would put me in ICU until I could go to a behavioral care center, where I would have to stay for a mandatory seventy-two hours. I said, "Okay, so be it."

I also had asked her if she could not tell my family that I'd tried to kill myself. And she said that that was doctor and patient confidentiality, so no, she wouldn't. My family got there then, and it was wonderful to see them again after I had felt and been so alone when I was dying. But I also felt guilty, like I'd failed them. And caused them to worry about me when I was busy just killing myself.

It was so complicated trying to learn how to kill myself, but it was very simple to learn how not to be suicidal, just by succeeding at it and learning that once you cross that line of no return and lose it all, that other people who still believe in life can give me a second chance. And that was all I had wanted and now had—a second chance.

I stayed in the ICU overnight, and then the next morning, two armed security guards came into my room and handcuffed me with zip ties. Luckily for me, my family had all gone back home and didn't have to see that. They led me across the parking lot to a smaller building that looked like it used to be a house. But there were lots of rooms inside. And one of them was mine. I had entered Aspen Hill.

I won't belabor that point, but I managed to get through all of the personal counseling and group therapy (with lots of cigarette breaks), and I did it all without letting myself get put on any psychiatric medications. Then I was finally let go and came back to Phoenix, where my car waited for me because my family had driven it back for me.

## Interlude Number 3

One time, I sugar-lowed as I was walking across the living room, and I dropped to my knees. I started crawling toward where my lunch box/cooler is because I kept an emergency glucose tube in there. But when I got to the cooler, I collapsed into it. My head went into the box, and the lid fell down on my neck. It wasn't big. The glucose tube fell out and slid away from my grasp.

I couldn't move anymore. I could barely think. All that I could think of was that this was it. This was how I was going to die. I was trapped, I couldn't breathe, and I was going to suffocate there on the floor with my head in the cooler. There just wasn't enough oxygen in the cooler. I started crying. I was so sad. But I didn't die. And I was embarrassed later when wiping away my tears. I hadn't suffocated. I hadn't died. And now I can laugh about it.

# CHAPTER NUMBER 4

From there, my current health insurance company informed me that since I had deliberately caused all of the current insurance claims, I had violated our "no suicide policy," and so they were cancelling my coverage, and all of the billing would go back to me, not the insurance company. So I was out of health insurance again. I hadn't read about the "no suicide policy."

And that was really bad timing because I got worse from there. My body now saw insulin as a threat of death and decided, out of a survival instinct, to fight insulin injections with histamine. Put bluntly, I became allergic to injected synthetic insulin. When I started taking synthetic insulin, it was because it was cheapest, but by then, it was all synthetic because it was cheapest.

I broke out in hives and rashes. I also got very itchy with the patches. And I had difficulty breathing when my throat started to swell up. I called my sister the first time it happened, and she drove me to the ER at John C. Lincoln hospital, a place that, over time with diabetes and all of its complications, would soon be like a second home.

At the ER, they validated that I had had an allergic reaction, but they couldn't tell what to. They just gave me a Benadryl injection and then let me go home. So from there, I started taking one-hundred-milligram tablets of generic Benadryl six times per day. But they made me so sleepy; I might as well have been drugged and/or knocked out.

I had already quit my job once I lost my insurance because I only stayed employed there for the insurance loophole. From there, I had gotten a new job at a rival company in the same industry. But there was no insurance with this new job. And now I quit this new job because I couldn't stay awake on the medication to go to work.

From there, I soon had my car repossessed, and had to move out of my apartment before the lease was up and then sleep on the couch of some friends. I found myself wishing that I had stayed dead from the insulin overdose because everything had gotten so much worse. I felt like I was reaping what I had sown, and it was all bad, bad karma.

All, except the way I got new insurance. My medical bills at the hospital were larger than the income I had, since I had no income, and that is how a person qualifies for the state health insurance (for poor people). So I did qualify and got Arizona Health Care Cost Containment System (AHCCCS). So that was something good.

After another especially bad sugar-low, the firefighters had the paramedics take me in the ambulance back to the hospital, where they admitted me into a room. The next day, the doctor told me that I could see an allergist (allergy specialist) if a doctor referred me to see one. I said, "Definitely," and so he did refer me.

Actually, he referred me to see an endocrinologist, a diabetic specialist, and that doctor referred me to see the allergist doctor. So it took a couple of months to finally see an allergist, but I finally did. He did the "back panel" tests for all known things that a person could be allergic to, but I wasn't allergic to any of them.

I asked him about insulin, and he told me that there was no test for insulin yet, so he couldn't tell. He said that there were only two other people allergic to insulin in the world, a lady in Europe and a lady in South America. But here in the United States, there were none on record. But, he said, next year there will be because I'm going to get in the medical journals for my insulin allergy.

The only answer for the allergy was better pills, ones that didn't knock me out nor even make me sleep, and then I'd just have to wait it out. Some allergies leave like they first showed up, all on their own and for no known reason. Many allergies leave within five years of their showing up. I couldn't believe five years, but it was true. Within five years, I stopped having allergic reactions and was off of the antihistamines.

## INTERLUDE NUMBER 4

One time, I went to take a shower, but I was too tired to stand up that long. That should have been my wake-up call. Instead, I took a bath and then blacked out during the bath. I didn't know it until later when I woke up. The water was cold. I was cold. But there wasn't much water left in the tub, only a couple of inches. The stopper was still over the drain, so I knew that it hadn't drained out.

Then I looked over the edge of the tub and saw that the floor was covered in water. And out in the hallway, the carpet was wet too. That is why the tub was almost empty. I had probably "seizured" during my sugar-low blackout and splashed most of the water out, which prevented me from drowning though. So it all worked out. And now I can laugh about it.

# CHAPTER NUMBER 5

During those five years, I had so many sugar-lows; it became a daily thing. If I didn't sugar-low one day, then I'd sugar-low that night, and then it'd be two to a day. So the average was one sugar-low per day for many years; hence, my plethora of sugar-low interludes. It was so difficult to regulate my glucose levels when my body fought the insulin that was supposed to be the answer to diabetes.

On one job, I had strained my stomach muscles so badly that I got a hernia. My employer paid the worker's compensation for the $5,000 it cost to have surgery. But I was so worried about being unconscious while they operated, with my diabetes, I opted for an epidural.

I lay on my side and then curled up to create spaces between my vertebrae. Then the doctor gave me an injection into my spine that numbed me from the waist down, covering the site of my hernia. A hernia occurs when too much strain is awkwardly put on the abdominal muscles, and they tear apart.

To fix it, an incision is cut into the skin over the tear, which is visible because where it's torn, the intestines poke through like a big skin bubble. Once the incision is sliced into the skin, it's separated, and a piece of plastic mesh is sewn through the muscle tissue and the mesh, holding the intestines inside once again. But right after my surgery, because I hadn't had anesthesia, I was wide awake.

So the nurse in charge of post-operation (post-op) thought I had taken longer to wake up and thought that I was ready to walk. In order to be released, the patient has to walk and then urinate to prove they're all right. So the nurse helped me stand up, then she started to let me go, not knowing that even though I was awake, my legs were still numb.

Luckily, for me, another nurse came into the post-op right then, just before she let me go, and he yelled at her, "Stop! Don't let go of him!" Oh, it was such a close call. That fall would've surely ripped my new stitches, and we would have to do it all over again, plus how much more.

It takes up to a month for the sutures to heal up completely. But for me, after a month at home on worker's compensation (which is 60 percent of your normal pay), I returned to the doctor, but he said that I hadn't healed at all during that month. We finally put it together that because of my diabetes and my sugars usually high, the stitching couldn't heal properly.

So they extended my compensatory (comp) time another month, and I tried to keep my sugars lower. In the end, it was all right, but I've never known pain like that post-op pain, which ended up lasting almost two months.

## Interlude Number 5

One time, I was sugar-lowing, and had just come home, and was changing into kick back clothes. But I had just got my pants around my ankles when I blacked out and fell forward, coming to a rest with my nose in a corner of the closet. That's how I was standing when the paramedics came into my room and saw me. One of them said, "Well, at least you have some clothes on this time." Because there were many times they came to rescue me, and found me completely naked. So sure, it was embarrassing then, but I can laugh about it now.

# CHAPTER NUMBER 6

The next big medical emergency that happened was that I broke my back. It had started out as a normal workday. Except that I had been fighting a cold and so I had had high sugars every time that I had checked my blood that day. And so each time that my sugars were still high, I took a correlating amount of insulin to bring it down. By the end of the day, I had worked a whole shift then came home and was kicking back. I was unable to eat supper because of my high sugars, and so I just took five more units of insulin and then sat down to drink three leftover Coronas from the night/weekend before. It was a Monday.

After all of the high sugars that I had had, I wasn't expecting my sugars to suddenly drop. But they did, and I blacked out sitting there. It turned into a very bad sugar-low, the second worst one, second only to dying in Flagstaff. Then I started to seizure. I had "spasmed" so badly that I broke three vertebrae.

Somehow, without "sugaring up," I still regained consciousness and carefully stood up. Boy, did I hurt something fierce! I texted my sister, whom I was staying with, but she was at a concert where one of her coworkers was singing in a competition. So I called my other sister, who came and got me in their car. She took me back to their apartment, and I lay down to rest because of the pain.

It boggles my mind now, knowing what was wrong with me, that I was doing all that activity even though I was that close to severing my spine. I could've become paralyzed so easily. I hurt so badly in my heart that my sister and her family were afraid that I'd had a heart attack. They finally called 911, and when the firefighters showed up and checked me out, they were also afraid that I had had a heart attack.

They called the paramedics, who put me on a gurney, and then put me in an ambulance. They drove me to the ER at my home away from home, John C. Lincoln hospital. I was going to be there for ten days. I sure didn't know that going in. From my arrival, they were looking out for a heart attack. But my heart was just fine. It took them two days to find out what had happened.

They x-rayed me, but nothing showed up. They gave me a computed tomography (CT) scan, but again, nothing showed up. Then they gave me a magnetic resonance imaging (MRI) and finally found out why they were giving me liquid morphine since I rolled in there. I had burst-fractured three vertebrae—T4, T5, and T6—all thoracic, including the ribs that they were connected to. And so, around front, my ribs hurt over where my heart was; hence the pain there.

I had also broken my left arm, about one inch below the shoulder. Now that they finally knew what was wrong, it was time to fix it. I was given a sponge bath and then shaved on my back because I'm like a yeti. I now have a 12″×1′ scar running down my spine. After making the incision on my back, they inserted Harrington rods to support the vertebrae and connecting ribs.

Then they stapled the incision together with forty-four metal staples into my skin. They couldn't and didn't do anything with my broken arm. From there, I got put into ICU because they couldn't balance out the highs and lows of my sugar-lows, just like I couldn't on my own. I stayed in the ICU several more days, then back to a "normal" room to finish out the rest of my ten-day stay in the hospital. I was released with a cane to help me balance when I walked.

## Interlude Number 6

One time, I was already sugar-lowing, and my friend, Daniel, drove us in his car to Taco Bell. I was talking a mile a minute nonstop. My friend ordered food for everyone in his family and for myself. When we got the food through the drive-through window, he handed me a burrito and told me to eat it. I did what he said and started eating it.

But after I had finished the burrito, my sugars had dropped low enough that I blacked out. I woke up much later back at his house on a living room couch. I said, "Hey! How did I get here? The last thing I knew I was just eating a burrito."

My friend's wife said, "Daniel! Did you just give him a burrito full of slowly digesting sugar instead of a quicker soda? Because that's messed up if you did."

Daniel said, "Well, at least he's been quieter the last few hours, hasn't he?"

Well, it was true, and now, I can laugh about it.

# CHAPTER NUMBER 7

The doctor who had performed my surgery told me that I had the thin, weak, brittle bones of a sixty-year-old woman because I had osteoporosis, which usually affects postmenopausal women. I had no idea why nor how I had developed osteoporosis. With osteoporosis, now it made sense for all of the other times that I had broken bones when it normally wouldn't have made sense.

There was one time when we had a downstairs neighbor who was a drug dealer, and when he and his "friends" were partying, they'd play their music way too loud and very late. So one night, at about two in the morning, I lost it and jumped up and down on the floor while yelling for them to shut up.

But I actually only jumped up and down once though because after that, my foot hurt too badly. The next day, I couldn't walk, so I couldn't go to work, so I went to the ER instead. There, they confirmed that I had broken my heel. And now it makes sense why it was so easy to break. I limped in pain for a whole year before my foot finally healed.

Another time, at work, I was drilling holes into steel but with a bit made for drilling in wood. So the grooves kept biting into the steel and jerking my hands. We were at the end of a job, so they wouldn't order new stuff, so we had to make-do with what we had. The bit finally bit into the steel too hard and jerked my wrists so badly that I broke the last two fingers on my right hand.

I reported it to my foreman, but he didn't think it was that bad, so he just let it go. But the next morning, my right hand was swollen and black, and my foreman knew he'd been wrong. He then reported it to the general foreman, but he did the same thing and told me to check back with him the next day.

So the next morning, I showed him my hand again, which was now swollen more and blacker. But he knew that they had waited too long to report it then, so he just transferred our whole crew to a job site where, due to a lawsuit, we had to be there, but we couldn't work. So that gave my fingers time to heal with just a hand brace. Now it makes sense why I broke my fingers when no one else did. It was osteoporosis.

I also, after having good teeth since childhood, all of a sudden started breaking teeth left and right. I broke four teeth, somewhat broken off or broken all the way down to the gum line. And like a doctor soon told me, teeth are bones too. And that's why they were breaking off. It was osteoporosis.

Like I wrote at the beginning, I used to be 6'2" tall (six feet, two inches). But now I am 5'11½" tall (five feet, eleven and a half inches tall), so I lost two and a half inches from my height due to osteoporosis.

## INTERLUDE NUMBER 7

One time, I was with my friend Daniel again. We were working at a job in California and sleeping in a motel. One night, I sugar-lowed while I was sleeping and woke up disoriented. But I knew what I needed to do. There were cans of soda in the little refrigerator in the kitchenette, so I got up to go to it.

But when I stood up, my head swam, and I collapsed to the floor. I started walking on my knees toward the fridge and bumped into Daniel, who was sleeping on the floor. I got major rug burns on my knees dragging along like that, but I finally got to the fridge. I grabbed a can of regular soda and started to open it, but then the tab broke off.

I loudly blurted out the f-bomb, "F——!"

At that, Daniel, who had woken up when I had bumped him, got up and came into the kitchenette with me. He opened another can of soda for me, and I started drinking. The rug burns hurt me for several days, but now I can laugh about it.

# Chapter Number 8

When I first left the hospital, I had a home care nurse visiting the apartment once a week. The first time he was going to visit, I was trying to shower and get dressed before he got there, but I had extremely sharp, stabbing pain in my left shoulder blade. It was so bad, as I was trying to put a shirt on, that I actually started crying. I was still crying when the nurse came in, and I told him I didn't know why it hurt so badly there.

He told me that it was a muscle spasm. He said that as my vertebrae got humped up higher than it used to be with the metal support system in there, that the back muscles stretching over it were now stretched thinner and tighter. And that is what causes the muscles to spasm, and thereby the pain.

But the muscle relaxer that I needed, it turned out that I already had, so I just had to take a pill and then lie down with a heating pad, and soon after, the pain faded away. But when the muscles did spasm, they hurt worse than the bone pain. It was injury upon injury.

## Interlude Number 8

One time, I sugar-lowed while kicking back at home in the evening. The only sugar source I had was a big chocolate bar I had put in the freezer to chill. But by then, it had frozen solid. I bit hard into it, and bit my way through a square of chocolate. But by the time that I had done that, I had blacked out.

But then, the sugar from the chocolate square kicked in, and I woke up groggily. I took another bite, ate another square, and then blacked out again. This went on for a couple of hours until I finally finished the whole chocolate bar. Then I finally had consumed enough sugar to stay awake. But my once white T-shirt was covered in melted chocolate smears from when I would break the pieces off. But now I can laugh about it.

# CHAPTER NUMBER 9

At one point—I know it's an interlude, but I haven't written it yet, so anyway—at one point, my back hurts so much more than usual that I'd just spent the whole day lying in bed, flat on my back, until I finally just gripped my hands into fists and pushed my fists into my forehead. Then I just cried. And my tears ran down into my ears. It was the worst pain that I had felt since I first broke my back.

I was already thinking about going to the hospital, and then my sisters said that I should go, so we made the decision to do it. When I got there, I was admitted into a room right away. Then I was given an MRI, and a neurologist studied the results. Then he came to my room and talked with my roommate while he studied me in secret.

Then he left and came back into the room to talk to me. He told me about studying me, and then he said that out of the osteoporosis, I had started developing osteoarthritis. And it was causing kyphosis in my back. Kyphosis is the normal curvature of the spine, but excessive is the beginning of a hunchback. With it, the bones hurt more, and the muscles spasm and hurt more.

He said that he could see me and my hunchback clearly and that it was pushing up from my thoracic into the cervical vertebrae, my neck. He said he could see me then unconsciously pushing my head up and back into my neck, making my posture horrible. From there, they sent a message to my regular doctor to get me started working with a pain management doctor, who then got me started in physical therapy. The physical therapist in the hospital had me learn to walk with a walker and then gave me a walker for my very own.

A day in the life of Bill: I have a prescription list of twenty-four, and eighteen of them are pills. I start the morning taking those pills. Then checking my blood sugars and taking a shot of insulin accordingly. During the night, I run out of all of my medications, and I wake up and get up in a world of hurt. It takes a good hour for the new pills to kick in.

During that time, I just drink coffee and watch the morning news shows. Then, when the coffee pot is empty, I take a bath to soak away the rest of the pain while the pills kick in some more. I had started off on Vicodin, then went to Norcos, and now I'm onto Oxycodone. Along with a muscle relaxer and two more support pills for pain.

From there, I can start laundry, wash dishes from the night before, or clean up some of the apartment. But I can only do some activities for about twenty minutes or so before I start hurting again. Then I have to stop what I'm doing and lie down to rest my back, to recuperate. This lasts for at least the rest of the hour. I was given a transcutaneous electrical nerve stimulator (TENS) unit for use for pain.

It has tabs that are wired to a little computer, and the tabs are stuck onto the areas of pain, resulting in an electric stimulation that helps ease the pain and release endorphins to help one feel better. Of course there's always a good ol' heating pad to help heal aches and pains in both muscle and bones. I can't even sit down for long without hurting. Lying down is best.

I was also diagnosed with degenerative disk disorder, or spondylosis, where my disks between the vertebrae are worn down and skinnier. That's in my lumbar area. My worst pain is in my lower back. But it hurts all the way up from my tailbone into my neck. That's all spine-centered, but I also have pain around the front of my ribs still, just like in the beginning.

After resting for at least an hour, I can get kind of busy again and mow the lawn or pull weeds in the garden, so long as I keep the activities around twenty minutes and then rest for the rest of the hour. I can stand up long enough to shower, but I prefer to take baths for the pain's sake, read, relax, and come out better for it. I even shave in the tub with a little hand mirror to save time standing in front of the mirror.

Other than working out in the yard, I don't get out of the house much, just doctor's appointments, where I hurt afterward—really badly, depending on how long the appointment takes. I rarely go to the grocery store and have to ride one of the motorized carts while I'm there. And then once in a while I'll make it to the library.

Following the twenty-minute rule, I can also cook meals and then kick back and watch TV in the evenings while I write. The best time for me is at night when I just lie down completely, and on my side, I curve my back, creating gaps between the vertebrae and resting without pain. So there's a day in the life of Bill.

## INTERLUDE NUMBER 9

One time, I was making lunch and had made a box of macaroni and cheese, but my sugars had dropped while I was cooking. By the time I had finished, I was pretty far gone. I walked out of the kitchen and toward the living room to eat when my left arm, which was holding the bowl of food, spasmed, and I dumped the whole bowl of mac and cheese onto the cat food dish.

From there, I just sat down on the couch with the empty bowl and blacked out. I woke up a bit later and looked at the empty bowl and wondered where the food had gone. I went back into the kitchen to see if I had left it in the pot, but then I saw what was left of the mac and cheese in the cat's dish. It was a bad lunch then, but now I can laugh about it.

# CHAPTER NUMBER 10

From there, my problems went internal. It started with something showing up on my blood work. So from there, I had an abdominal sonogram, then a CT scan, then an abdominal MRI. My primary care physician, a nurse practitioner, had already told me that I had an enlarged left atria in my heart. And now she said that my liver was swollen, my right kidney was swollen, as well as my prostate, and my spleen. I also had six cysts on my right kidney and seven tumors on my liver.

The CT scan wasn't as bad as the MRI. It's just a big ring that I lay down in partway and it takes pictures. I felt a little trapped, but it's not that bad. The sonogram was even easier. It was just like it looks on TV when pregnant women see their babies. There's a slippery lubricant on my belly, and the sonogram tool slides around taking pictures of my internal organs. Only problem there was that it was with a guy.

I could see them one at a time on a black-and-white monitor, like my kidney. It was interesting. But the MRI was scary. It's a big cylinder, and you lay completely inside. Now, I'm claustrophobic, and to be inside a tight cylindrical machine that runs right in front of your face—I barely had breathing room. And it's loud: *Ka-chunk! Ka-chunk!* Over and over!

And it takes a long time; I was in there for two forty-five-minute sessions—an hour and a half. In fact, I panicked at one point and hit the emergency stop button. And they soon let me out. I just breathed a big sigh of relief! But then after just a bit, I had to go back in and finish it.

After all of that, my nurse told me that she can't diagnose me with cancer. An oncologist would have to do that. So she might as well have told me that I do have cancer. I got several referrals to see specialists for all of my problems: heart, prostate, kidney with hypertension (high blood pressure), and an oncologist, plus a specialist for heartburn.

The best thing was the kidney and hypertension specialist because that doctor told me that with high blood pressure, the kidneys can't metabolize calcium correctly, and that results in osteoporosis. So now I know how I developed osteoporosis, even though I'm a younger guy versus an older woman.

I got new prescriptions for medications for all of these different things (which I've already gotten into), and they did what they're supposed to, so I got better in every area—including for the cancer. The swelling went down in my heart, liver, right kidney, prostate, and spleen.

Plus the cysts on my right kidney and the tumors on my liver all faded to lesions, then those faded away to nothing, except one seven millimeter benign cyst. I was problem free and cancer free! Whew! The weird thing was, though, that at that time, I was still being charged co-pays for my prescription medications, but I couldn't afford more, so I didn't do those new medications until much later when they dropped my co-pays. So how did I get free of so many bad things without the proper medications?

## Interlude Number 10

One time, I was making supper, but then I sugar-lowed and my left arm spasmed again, and I spilled a pot of food all over the counter and floor. We ended up eating ramen noodles for supper. But now I can laugh about it.

# CHAPTER NUMBER 11

I also, due to my seizures and being diagnosed with a seizure disorder, got a referral to see a neurologist. And she referred me to, and scheduled me for, a study at Banner Good Samaritan hospital. It was a horrible thing. I was scheduled for a five-day stay, but it turned into nine days and was only that because I attempted to run away from the hospital before they released me (AMA: against medical advice).

But anyways, it started with me buzzing my head bald, with hair-trimming clippers, at home by myself. Then I checked in at the hospital where they gave me a brain MRI first. Then they glued (literally) sensor pads to my scalp, thirty-five of them. Off each of them was a wire that all hooked up to a computer.

Then they put me in a bed and buckled me in with a leather belt. Then they padlocked the leather belt to lock me into the bed. I could only leave the bed when they unlocked me to go to the restroom while a nurse watched me. No privacy whatsoever. They even had cameras in the room that stayed on me in the bed and then followed me to and from the restroom.

I watched TV, read, and tried to nap for five straight days, while they monitored me to see if I seizured and, if I did, which parts of my brain were affected by the seizure. They were trying to see if I was epileptic or just hypoglycemic due to brittle diabetes. It was itchy, uncomfortable, invasive of my privacy, and I hated it.

By the end of the five days, they used turpentine to cut the acetone glue on my scalp and, one by one, unhooked all of the sensors. They didn't let me go home from there though. I went from there to another "regular" room and finally showered after the five days without getting clean. I shaved too of course. It felt good.

While I was there, they also had me talk with a psychiatrist, and then that turned into five psychiatrists during the five days. That's one of the reasons why they wanted to keep me there longer. They also had trouble keeping my blood sugar levels regulated, and so they wanted to work with me more.

My sugars would rush up to four hundred plus and then inexplicably crash back down to below fifty just as fast. The roller coaster wouldn't stop. They finally had to diagnose me with brittle diabetes. They couldn't blame me for it anymore. That's why I left; I couldn't stand the four hundreds anymore, so I made a run for the elevators with my two suitcases. But they caught me at the elevator and convinced me to come back in for another couple of days.

In the meantime, the psychiatrists were busy. They gave me a number of psychological tests and graded me accordingly. They also interviewed me thoroughly and counseled me exhaustingly. There was a lot of therapy. They diagnosed me with post-traumatic stress disorder (PTSD), borderline personality disorder, bipolar, depression and anxiety disorder, plus obsessive compulsive disorder (OCD).

Then they started me on psychotropic medications for all of the disorders, and so I had five new meds. They also put in my application to the State of Arizona for Serious Mental Illness (SMI), which I was soon approved for. Then I got into regular therapy, then in-home therapy, plus seeing a psychiatrist once every month for my prescriptions.

## INTERLUDE NUMBER 11

One time, I was sleeping over at my foreman's house with his family. They had really nice furniture. In fact, he told me that his wife had told him that even he couldn't sleep on the couch. But one evening that he and his family went out to eat, I was tired, and I fell asleep on their couch. Then I sugar-lowed while I slept, and I even peed on the couch.

It is common to urinate when a diabetic has a hypoglycemic episode. And I did it often, I'm embarrassed to admit. When my foreman and his family came home, his family went to their bedrooms, and he stayed out in the living room with me while he called 911 for the paramedics.

In California, the paramedics are actual EMTs in an ambulance. They came and helped me sugar up even though before they got there, I tried crawling to my cooler to where I had an emergency glucose tube. But my foreman wouldn't help me. I think that he was more afraid than I was. The next morning, my foreman's wife started cleaning up the couch cushions from my pee. It was horrible. But now I can chuckle about it.

# CHAPTER NUMBER 12

In the meantime, I've been going to my pain management doctor for several years, every month for my pain meds prescriptions, plus, along the way, I got spinal injections for the pain, and they hurt worse than the bone pain was. I'd lie down on my stomach, and the doctor was busy on my back, inserting long needle injections into the joints of the vertebrae, six at a time.

They never worked though, so it was all a waste of time, unfortunately. So they settled for the last resort—nerve burning. It's where they electronically burn the nerves where it hurts so that you can't feel the pain anymore. It's also a painful process, injecting long needles into the joints of the vertebrae and then moving them all around.

Those nerve burnings did work but not for long. They're supposed to last from three months to five years, but they would only last up to two months for me, and then I'd be hurting again. So then they'd have to wait six months before they did it again, and then the doctor would inject deeper and move them around more to burn more nerves. It might last three months that time, but that was it.

## INTERLUDE NUMBER 12

One time, I was staying at my friend Daniel's house, and I started sugar-lowing when he and his family were all gone. I started heating up some soup in the microwave, but then it got too hot, and I couldn't eat it. Then my low sugars made me collapse, and I fell to the floor. I crawled across the kitchen floor to the telephone and called 911. That was the first time that I ever called 911 on my own.

I couldn't even speak when they answered the phone, and I just hoped that the address showed up on the computer on their end. It did, and when they came to the trailer house to help me, I was blacked out on the kitchen floor. The paramedics hooked me up to an IV and got some sugar in me. Then I came back around.

The firefighters said that they couldn't believe that I had sugar-lowed, when on the kitchen table, three feet away from where I lay, there were twenty something Easter baskets full of candies. But I told them that I had been told specifically not to eat any of the candies. They were counted out and called for. Even they laughed about that one then.

# Chapter Number 13

S o like I had said before, I had worked the day that I broke my back, *but* I haven't worked even one day since then. I just haven't been able to. If there was a job for mattress testers, then I could do that, but that's it. It is only by the good graces of my family that I've survived this long. But, of course, I've applied for social security disability, but so far, not so good.

It took a while for me to apply for it in the first place. I had been told by both of my parents, who both died while waiting for disability. And so I had no faith in it. But then, a good friend of the family, who, it turns out, had broken his back and got approved for disability, encouraged me to apply for it, and so I finally did.

It turned out to be the best timing too because that was the last month that I was qualified to apply for it. One more month, and it would have been too late. I feel like it was meant to be because of that. But who knows? At the very least, I did apply on time for it when I was still qualified to apply. Put simply.

I had seen a commercial on television for a company that helps people apply for disability, and so I called them before I applied. They were the ones who helped me apply online. I had to sign away 25 percent of the back pay/lump sum to them for it, but then they just disappeared and didn't help me anymore.

They had just helped me long enough to get their claws in me, and then they stopped helping. It took me months of their inactivity for me to track them down, and then I wrote a stern letter to their CEO, telling them to get me out from under their money grasping grip and let me go.

Then I continued dealing with social security on my own like I had done from almost the very first. And it was a lot of paperwork! And a lot of time. But after six months and two doctor appointments (medical and psychological), I finally got my answer—denied! But it wasn't over there. I appealed their decision and got the ball rolling for a second try.

But after another six months and a lot more paperwork, I got denied again. The first time I was denied, they just made it seem like I was lying. But the second time, they made it seem like all of the doctors were lying too. It was very ignorant of them to imply that. I got to thinking that my parents were probably right.

My dad had said that they were paid to say no! So when you deal with any of them, they're good at saying no. If they say yes, then the disabled are paid out of their former paycheck because they're fired! I was beginning to believe that, as paranoid as it might sound, my dad was probably right.

I appealed the second denial too, and then the Social Security Administration (SSA) strongly suggested that I have counsel for the next part. So I called another lawyer firm, but this time local, and got set up for the next step, which was a hearing before a federal judge.

I had to wait eighteen months for that hearing and then another two months to find out the result, and I got denied again. But my attorneys filed for another appeal, and now I have to wait another eighteen months for it.

## Interlude Number 13

One time, I had sugar-lowed in the evening at my sister's apartment. She had tried helping me sugar up, but I wouldn't cooperate, which is common for diabetics, unfortunately. So when she couldn't get enough sugar in me, she called 911 for the paramedics. But then I came back around from the sugar that I had drank, and so we didn't need firefighters anymore.

My sister told me to go outside and tell them that I was all right and that we wouldn't need their help. All I caught was "Go outside." I was really down. But I went even though I was complaining the whole time, "I can't believe you're kicking me out like this! What? Did I sugar-low one too many times now?"

"I don't even have my shoes on or my phone or my wallet. What am I supposed to do?"

But by then I had reached the parking lot and saw the firefighters and said to myself, *Hey, great! I can just use my sugar-low to get them to have an ambulance take me to the ER at the hospital!*

It was perfect timing. I didn't know that they were there for me in the first place. It turned out that I didn't have to go to the ER, and my sister let me back in her apartment. So what was very bad for our neighbor's mom wasn't bad for me, and so I can laugh about it now.

# Chapter Number 14

Along the way, on top of Aspen Hill, I ended up going to another behavioral health hospital. I had started the morning just going to a regular doctor appointment. But my regular doctor, who was a nurse practitioner, wasn't in the office that day. She had a substitute, another nurse practitioner.

She saw me, but as I brought up my struggles with my diabetes, she read in my file and then asked me about the suicide "attempt" from Flagstaff. I had to tell her that "yes, that had happened, but not since then." She asked me if maybe I was still trying to kill myself. I, again, said, "No, I wasn't." But she didn't believe me.

She told me that there were people at St. Luke's that I could talk to and then maybe go stay with them. I agreed to talk with them. But the people who showed up were two EMTs who brought a gurney with them and then strapped me onto it. They rolled me right out of the building and on to St. Luke's.

Once in there, they had me strip down naked in front of a nurse's aide, a man. And then they took my boot laces. They gave me a packet of stuff to shower and shave with and gave me a blanket and pillow for a bed in a room, where, thank God, I didn't have a roommate. I got in on time for lunch, and surprisingly, it was a whole lot of good food.

They even had a smoking area in the middle of the place that had no roof and was open to the sky. I was immediately and continually interviewed by psychotherapists, and then, of course, there was group therapy, which was pretty lame. But there was one girl (the campus was coed) whose problem was that she was five years old in her mind.

She wore onesie/footed pajamas and carried around a stuffed alligator and spoke in baby talk. She said, during her lucid moments in group therapy, that whenever she got stressed out or felt that she was in crisis, she would revert to the "little girl her." She was by no means the only one there with issues.

There was a twenty something white guy who claims that he was a pimp, drug dealer, and druggie who was trying to go cold turkey off of heroin. There was a Native American lady who was trying to go cold turkey off of alcohol, and she said, as a child, she and other kids in their families on the reservation were literally passed around the drunken partygoers like sex toys.

There was even a young Mexican man in a jail jumpsuit who told me that he cut himself to go there instead of being locked up in jail. And then there was my roommate, who moved in about two in the morning. He liked to walk around the whole place, not just our room, in his loose "tighty whiteys."

He kept his dentures in a cup in the restroom, which makes sense, but he forgot about it and then accused me of stealing them. And that was it! That was the straw that broke this camel's back. I wanted out, and I wanted out then! I had been watching a side door, and I could see that it wasn't locked.

And it was out of line of the main vision. And I still had my clothes, boots, and my cell phone. So all I'd be losing would be my boot laces, and I could always buy more of those. But then I thought about the fact that AHCCCS was paying for this, and if I ran away, they wouldn't be happy. Plus, I might get billed for it.

So I decided to talk to them about letting me leave. I asked them. But they said no. So I pushed it, and they went into panic mode. The lady that I was talking to called for two security guards. One stood by the door, and one stood by me. Then the lady in charge said, "You're assessed with subconsciously trying to kill yourself constantly. If we let you go, you'll kill yourself."

I told them that I hadn't broken any laws. I hadn't hurt anyone. I didn't deserve to be locked up. It was a prison for me. And I didn't deserve it. The lady in charge that morning called the psychiatrist that I hadn't even seen yet, and he told them to let me go. She and they couldn't believe it. But they had me sign some paperwork for release and then handed me my boot laces. And out the door I went.

## INTERLUDE NUMBER 14

One time, I had sugar-lowed in the kitchen and fell down on the floor on my back, hitting my head against the refrigerator. Then I started to seizure and repeatedly banged the back of my head against the fridge door. After I came to, I called my sister, and she took me to the ER. It turned out that I had gotten a concussion. Maybe I could laugh about it now, but I don't.

# CHAPTER NUMBER 15

So that about sums it up. From the beginning of a healthy lifestyle to a snowball effect of going from bad to worse to *the* worst. Plus a day in the life, as well as my social security disability struggles. And, yes, I've had my difficulties with suicidal behavior along the way, but I just wish that the failed experiments didn't make things worse, even though I've had to learn that I know that they don't make things better.

Maybe someone can learn from my mistakes though and not try the same or similar things in their lives. That would make it all worth it. Well, here's to better health and better lives!

### Extra "Episodes"

One time, I was sugar-lowing and thereby needed to sugar up, but I had too much back pain from when I had broken my back, and so I could barely move. I just lay down on my bed, gripped my hands into fists, and pressed my fists to my forehead, trying to deal with the pain. It was so bad, I started crying, and my tears ran down into my ears.

The tears in my ears were a new experience for me. I didn't laugh about it then, and I still haven't laughed about it since.

\*\*\*

One time, I was staying at my friend Daniel's house, and we were watching a Godzilla movie. I had wanted some alcoholic refreshments, but all my friend had was a partial bottle of mescal, which is a cousin to tequila, from his wedding. It's strong, and so no one had finished it for years.

We didn't have any limes to go with it nor chasers for after it, but we did have some "limon" salt, so I licked that before and after shots to help with the taste. All by myself, drinking straight shots, with no mixers or chasers, I drank sixteen shots of mescal, emptying the bottle. Then I checked my blood sugar levels and saw to my horror that I had a 362, which is very high! And I was very scared! I figured that the only reason that I had been able to drink that much hard liquor was because without insulin to lock it away, it had just stayed in my blood, not in my brain cells.

But now, I was going to have to take insulin to bring down the high sugars, and that will lock away the alcohol into my brain cells, and then who knows how heavy the intoxication is going to be? But I took the correlating amount of insulin and then sat back to wait, scared to death.

I got to thinking about 911, and I thought that for safety's sake, I needed to call 911 for the paramedics to take me to the hospital because I didn't want to risk dying from alcohol poisoning. My buddy didn't want to call 911, so he didn't, but then I did because I was too scared not to. It was just the second time I had called 911 on my own.

They said to me that I was just drunk and needed to sleep it off. And then I told them that they were the reason so many drunk people die in McKinley county because they don't give any value to people who are drunk. I accused them of being the cause that my brother, a police officer there, had to pick up so many suiciders.

Now, even though I hadn't threatened to commit suicide, just because I had said the word suicide, that was a red flag, and then they had to pick me up and take me to a hospital. So they sent a police officer to the house and handcuffed me and put me in the police car and took me to a hospital where my room was kept under watch.

I was just glad that I was finally in a hospital for safety's sake. And now, I can kind of chuckle about it somewhat.

***

One time, another time that I was taking a bath when I sugar-lowed, I seizured so wildly that I was already bruised up badly when the paramedics came to help me. That was one of the many times that I was naked when they came to help me. If I wanted to, I could laugh about it now.

***

One time, I sugar-lowed while asleep on the living room floor in my sister's apartment. I couldn't wake up when my sister tried to help me, so my sister called 911. And when the firefighters showed up, they resuscitated me, then pointed out that all around the blankets on the floor was black puke. A firefighter said that it was blood. I had thrown up black blood all around where I slept. That was a scary one. I never got to the bottom of that one. I've never laughed about it.

\*\*\*

One time, when the paramedics came to rescue me, I was lying underneath a heavy sliding rocking chair. I was tangled up into it, and my glasses were badly broken. The firefighters untangled me from the chair and got it off of me before they helped me recoup my sugars. After they had "reupped" my sugars, they then told me about my entanglement in the chair, and then they asked me how it had happened. I had no explanation or answer. But, in spite of my broken glasses at that time, now I can laugh about it.

\*\*\*

One time, when I was at work, my supervisor took me off of the floor at Cabelas and sent me outside by myself to clean up the entrance to the store by picking up cigarette butts. So I did that. But when break time came around, no one told me to take a break, so I didn't have the opportunity to check my blood sugar levels and keep myself regulated.

So it was no surprise that I sugar-lowed then. I wobbled, stumbled, and fell down, then rolled around on the ground. People walking into the store told employees inside, and they then told my supervisor. He came outside to check on me, saw what and how I was doing, then he told his supervisor that I was drunk or on drugs, or something like that, and I needed to be fired.

But my coworkers told him that "he isn't drunk nor on drugs. He's a diabetic, and he's probably sugar-lowing."

They came outside and got me up and back inside where they proceeded to get me a soda while the managers called 911 for paramedics. When I had stabled somewhat, I told them that my supervisor hadn't told me when break time was, and so, because he forgot me, I couldn't keep myself regulated. So they didn't fire me. And now I can laugh about it.